MW01294405

Warren Buffett

43 Lessons for Business & Life

Keith Lard

Table of Contents

Copyright © 2017 Keith Lard

All rights reserved. No part of this book may be reproduced
or transmitted in any form or by any means, electronic or
mechanical, including photocopying, recording or by any
information storage and retrieval system without written
permission of the publisher, except for the inclusion of brief
quotations in a review.

Introduction

There is something special about being considered one of the top investors in the world today. Buffett ranks among the list of not only the top investors of our time, but among the world's best of all time. Buffett has managed to rise to the top of the ranks in stellar fashion, confounding the critics and earning the adulation of millions.

The son of Howard and Leila Buffett, Warren Edward Buffett was born in Omaha, Nebraska on August 30, 1930. He is the second of three children and the only son of the Buffett's. As a child he attended Rose Hill Elementary School, showing early on a unique interest and skill in financial and business matters. The young Buffett had a knack for mathematics and was able to solve complicated numerical problems in his head. Even at a young age, Buffett was already dabbling in stock investments, with frequent visits to his father's stock brokerage office.

His first investment took place when he was just 11 years old. He purchased three shares of Cities Service Preferred, costing $38 each. The stock dipped to a low of $27, but Buffett still held on to the shares until they increased again, reaching $40 per share. He then sold the shares for a small profit, but later admitted regretting this decision especially as Cities Service shares eventually rose to around $200 each. He attributes this experience as one of his earliest lessons on the value of patience when engaging in investments.

Entrepreneurship also began at a young age. When he was six years old, he would buy six-packs of Coca Cola from a grocery store owned by his grandfather at 25 cents per pack, reselling them for a nickel each. He sold chewing gum and candies as well. Then came his own newspaper distribution business at the age of 13 as a paperboy, earning up to $5,000 by the time he graduated high school. That year, he filed his very first tax return, with a $35 tax deduction for his bike. He would also sell his own horseracing tip sheet to clients.

In 1942, Buffett's father was elected to his first term in the United States House of Representatives. The Buffett family relocated to Fredericksburg, Virginia. Warren attended the Woodrow Wilson High School, a secondary school located in Washington, D.C., whose notable alumni include television personality Alex Wagner, journalist Roger Mudd, news anchor Derek McGinty, Florida congressman Clifford Stearns, Muppets creator Jim Henson, and Ethernet co-inventor David Boggs.

While in high school, the entrepreneurial ventures continued. He and a friend pooled some money together to buy a used pinball machine for $25, which they installed in a local barbershop. After just a few months, the profits they earned from this first machine gave them enough money to purchase more machines in three other places in the D.C. area. Eventually, Buffett was able to sell the business for $1,200. His business ventures even at this age made it apparent to those around him that he would one day likely choose a career in business. His high school yearbook photo describes him as someone who "likes math: a future stock broker".

By the age of 15, Buffett was already making about $175 each month just from delivering Washington Post newspapers to subscribers. He was also able to invest some of his money into one of his father's businesses, and purchase a 40-acre farm. He graduated high school in 1947, at the age of 17 years old. He did not want to go to college initially. After all, he was already making money from his various ventures, particularly from his newspaper delivery business which had already raked in around $5,000 (or about $42,000 today). However, his father convinced him to attend college anyway.

Buffett enrolled at the Wharton School of Finance and Commerce, the business school of the University of Pennsylvania, located in Philadelphia. Wharton is one of the top business schools in the world, with its MBA and undergraduate programs consistently top-ranked by *Forbes, Business Insider, U.S. News and World Report*, and other publications. Buffett, however, did not particularly enjoy his stay at Wharton, and he often complained that he knew more than his professors. He only stayed at Wharton for two years. In 1949, he opted to move back to his hometown of Omaha, where he transferred to the University of Nebraska-Lincoln. He worked full-time while studying, but managed to graduate in only three years by taking some of his credits during the summer. He graduated with a Bachelor of Science in Business Administration at the age of 19. By this time, his various business enterprises had already given him a savings of $9,800 (equal to about $99,000 in today's valuation).

After completing his bachelor's degree, Buffett was encouraged to pursue graduate studies, an idea which he also did not care for. However, he was convinced to apply to Harvard Business School. The renowned institution, however, rejected his application because he was "too young". Feeling slighted by the rejection, Buffett then decided to instead enroll at the Columbia Business School of Columbia University, influenced by the book *The Intelligent Investor* by Benjamin Graham. His decision was influenced upon knowing that Graham himself was teaching at Columbia at the time, along with David Dodd, another famous investor.

During his time at Columbia, Buffett had the privilege of learning from Graham and Dodd. He found out that Graham was on the board of GEICO, an insurance company, and decided to go to the headquarters of GEICO one day to speak to one of the top-level executives of the company. As luck would have it, he was able to speak to the Financial Vice President, Lorimer Davidson. Buffett asked Davidson many questions about the insurance business, with the impromptu meeting lasting for hours.

Buffett was an exceptional student in his graduate studies at Columbia. It is said that he is the only student to ever garner an A+ in Graham's class. After graduate school, he started working at his father's company, the Buffet-Falk and Company, as an investment salesman. After finishing with a Master of Science in Economics, Buffett also attended the New York Institute of Finance, taking a public speaking course. Buffett also tried his hand at teaching an evening class on investment principles at the University of Nebraska-Omaha. Many of his students were much older than him, but he was able to hold his own. During this time, he invested in a Texaco gas station, which turned out to be his first unsuccessful venture.

Buffett was married to Susan Thompson in 1952, and their

first child Susan Alice was born the following year. In 1954, he was finally offered a position at the partnership of his mentor, Benjamin Graham. Graham had opposed the idea of Buffett working at Wall Street immediately after graduate school, and had turned down Buffett's offer years earlier to work at his firm for free. But Buffett eventually was offered a job as a securities analyst for Graham-Newman Corporation, with a salary of $12,000 yearly (or about $107,000 in today's valuation). During his time at Graham-Newman, he worked with Walter Schloss, a noted fund manager and investor. Also in 1954, Warren and Susan's second child, Howard Graham, was born.

Until 1956, Buffett steadily grew his personal capital to around $174,000 ($1.53 million in today's valuation) from his various income streams. Suddenly Graham decided to retire and close his partnership. This prompted Buffett to move back to Omaha and start his own firm. He spoke to seven partners, among them his sister Doris and his aunt Alice, raised $105,000 in capital, and created Buffett Associates, Ltd. Buffett's firm used many of the techniques he had picked up from his time being mentored by Graham. He zeroed in on undervalued companies and invested in them, and before 1956 ended, his partnership was already managing about $300,000 in capital funds. He bought a five-bedroom house in

Omaha, where he still resides to this day, for $31,500, and managed his partnership from his home office.

Soon, Buffett's business empire grew to several other partnerships. By 1960, he was operating seven successful partnerships, and became a millionaire by 1962. Capital had grown to $7.2 million, and Warren had over 90 limited partners all over the United States. Buffett's partnerships were averaging a 251% profit, at a time when the Dow's was up around 74.3%. The same year he became a millionaire, he decided to merge all of his partnerships into a single entity.

He next set his sights on a big textile manufacturing company, Berkshire Hathaway. The firm was founded in 1839 by Oliver Chace in Rhode Island. In 1962, Buffett started purchasing Berkshire Hathaway stocks after he took note of the stock's price trajectory whenever a company-owned mill closed. However, Buffett soon conceded that the textile firm was declining, and Hathaway's Seabury Stanton tendered an offer of $11 and 1/2 per share for the company to buy back shares from Buffett, to which he agreed. However, when the offer was tendered in writing, the price was only for $11 and 3/8 per share, which angered Buffett. In an aggressive move, he decided to purchase more of Berkshire Hathaway's stocks, seized control of the company, and fired Stanton.

With the takeover, Buffett found himself with a textile

manufacturing company on the decline. During the first few years, he still continued the textile manufacturing part of the business, but soon started to expand Berkshire Hathaway into other industries and investments. One of the first was Berkshire's purchase of National Indemnity Company, an insurance company also based in Omaha, and the acquisition of an equity stake in the Government Employees Insurance Company or GEICO. Warren phased out Berkshire's textile manufacturing in 1985, but expanded its investments into The Washington Post, Exxon, Coca-Cola, Salomon Brothers, Wells-Fargo, Apple, IBM, United Airlines, Delta Air Lines, Southwest Airlines, and American Airlines.

Currently, Berkshire Hathaway fully owns GEICO, Fruit of the Loom, Net Jets, Long and Foster, Dairy Queen, Lubrizol, BNSF Railway, Pampered Chef, and FlightSafety International. Forbes Global 2000 ranks Berkshire Hathaway as the third biggest public company worldwide, and the world's ninth-largest multinational conglomerate in terms of revenue, at $223.60 billion in 2016. The company has subsidiaries in virtually every industry, including construction (Acme Brick Company), luxury jewelry (Ben Bridge Jeweler, Borsheim's Fine Jewelry, Helzberg), media (Business Wire, The Buffalo News), clothing (Brooks Sports, Fechheimer Brothers Company), and many more.

A notable investment of Berkshire Hathaway was its purchase of stocks in the Coca-Cola Company in the late 1980's. Buffett started purchasing Coca-Cola stocks in 1988, and soon controlled up to 7% of the company, with an investment worth $1.02 billion. This investment is still considered to be among the most successful and lucrative investments of Buffett. Not long after, as Berkshire Hathaway began selling class A shares, Buffett officially became a billionaire on May 29, 1990. Buffett became company director, and also served as director for The Gillette Company, Citigroup Global Markets Holdings, and Graham Holdings Company.

Buffett's career has not been without significant controversies. Notably, in 1974 the Securities and Exchange Commission (SEC) investigated Berkshire Hathaway's purchase of Wesco Financial, a California-based diversified financial firm. This was due to a perceived conflict of interest, although no charges were filed. Three years later, when Berkshire invested into the Buffalo Evening News in a $32.5 million deal, its competitor Buffalo Courier-Express filed antitrust charges. The Courier-Express eventually went out of business in 1982. Another crisis that Buffett had to weather was the scandal involving John Gutfreund, a former CEO of Salomon Brothers of which Berkshire Hathaway had purchased a 12% stake. Buffett's firm was the largest shareholder, and he was a director of Salomon Inc. In 1990, it was discovered that a trader, Paul Mozer, was submitting bids on behalf of Salomon Brothers beyond what was permitted by the U.S. Treasury. The actions of Mozer had been reported to Gutfreund, then the CEO of Salomon, but he did not immediately take action. The ensuing scandal forced Gutfreund to leave the company in 1991, and Buffett assumed chairmanship of Salomon during the difficult period.

During the subprime mortgage crisis of 2007-2008, the precursor to the 2007 global recession, Buffett was also heavily criticized for what many perceived as Berkshire's involvement in many of the subprime deals, particularly in allocating capital too early on that facilitated many of the deals. In an opinion piece for The Wall Street Journal, Peter Eavis wrote that while Buffett has been lauded for many brilliant deals, it may be time for him to "get a new crystal ball".

"Mr. Buffett looks to be committing his capital too early. On some bets, waiting might have gotten him better terms or more attractive entry prices," Eavis said. Eavis called out Berkshire's default protection for some North American corporations which had junk ratings, exposing itself to millions of dollars' worth of losses in credit default swaps. "Berkshire more than doubled its national exposure on these CDS to $8.8 billion between the end of 2006 and the middle of this year," according to Eavis. "Given the deterioration in the credit markets, the third quarter hit on them could be large." Berkshire Hathaway did suffer significant losses during the 2007 recession, particularly a 77% earnings decrease reported during the third quarter of 2008. Many of Berkshire's deals also suffered huge market losses. One of the more publicized moves of Berkshire during this time was its acquisition of 10% perpetual preferred stock of Goldman Sachs, a multinational finance company heavily involved in the subprime mortgage crisis. Berkshire purchased preferred stock worth $5 billion, and warrants to purchase another $5 billion common stock within a 5-year period.

A significant milestone was reached by Buffett's Berkshire Hathaway on August 14, 2014 when the company's shares were valued at $200,000 each. This capitalized Berkshire Hathaway at $328 billion, of which Buffett had 321,000 shares or about $64.2 billion. Six days later, Berkshire Hathaway was ordered to pay a fine of $896,000 for its failure to report a December 2013 purchase of shares in USG Corporation.

Aside from his many investment achievements, Buffett's personal life has also drawn much interest among followers of his. Buffett has three children with his deceased first wife Susan, although the couple encountered marital problems and lived separately from 1977 until Susan's death in 2004. On

Warren's 76th birthday, he married his long-time partner Astrid Menks, who had been his companion since his separation from his wife.

Curiously, Buffett claimed in a 2006 interview that he does not have a chauffeur, preferring to drive himself around. The wealthy investment mogul also says he does not carry around a mobile phone, does not have a computer on his home office desk, eschews an entourage when travelling, and has only ever sent one e-mail his whole life. He does read about five newspapers each day, including the Berkshire-owned Omaha World Herald. He still lives in the same Omaha home he purchased in 1958, although he also has a house in Laguna Beach, California worth $4 million.

For relaxation, Buffett follows Nebraska football games avidly, attending as many of the games as possible. He also likes to play bridge with his friend Bill Gates, reportedly playing up to 12 hours every week and even sponsoring a nationwide bridge tournament.

Many enthusiasts follow Warren's speeches, which are known to be humor-filled, folksy, but memorable. Buffett still presides over the annual shareholder meeting of Berkshire Hathaway, which is held in Omaha's Qwest Centre. The annual meeting is attended by over 20,000 people from all over the world, and has been dubbed the "Woodstock of

Capitalism" because of its popularity.

In these speeches, and in many other interviews, anecdotes, publications, and other quotes from Warren Buffett, you will see an enigmatic, unique, insightful investment magnate with plenty to share and wisdom to impart. As a leader, entrepreneur, potential investor, student, or whatever your calling may be, you stand to learn from the many life lessons of one of the most successful investors of all time, and one who is still very active and at the top of his game. In the following pages, let us delve into the different philosophies on life, finance, business, investment, savings, and other aspects of living, as seen by Warren Buffett.

Chapter One: Warren Buffett's Investment Insights

Warren Buffett has been given the nickname the "Oracle of Omaha", as he resides in the Nebraskan city and has proven to be quite insightful when it comes to picking which investments would yield gains down the road. The term "Oracle" has also become quite the appropriate moniker for Buffett. His comments on the market and global economy, as well as beliefs on aspects of investment, business, and life in general, are closely followed by his ardent disciples who hang on to his every word. And for good reason, it would be foolish not to learn from a man who has accomplished so much.

So, what are some of these memorable quotes from the "Oracle of Omaha"? Let us look at some of his advice, quotes, and comments regarding investing, where he is undoubtedly considered one of the foremost experts:

Lesson #1

"The best thing that happens to us is when a great company gets into temporary trouble... We want to buy them when they're on the operating table."

When Buffett was quoted by Anthony Bianco, a senior correspondent for Bloomberg BusinessWeek, giving the statement above in 1999, he was explaining what value investing is all about. It is waiting on the side lines for a solid, profitable company to experience certain financial problems or have a need for cash. It is at this moment an investor can then pounce on the opportunity to purchase stocks, generally at heavily discounted prices.

Successful value investing requires you to be aware of the trends, reports, and earnings of a company whose stock you are eyeing. The general trend is for a publicly traded company's stock prices to decrease when it is experiencing some upheaval, difficulty, or challenging period, and this is a window of opportunity to purchase stock and invest in an otherwise stable and reliable company at great prices. In time, when the situation normalizes again, and the stock price goes up, you will find yourself getting back what you put in, and then earning more.

Lesson #2

"Risk comes from not knowing what you are doing."

Risk is a part of the business world, and while there is no way to completely eliminate risk, there are ways to research what the risks are, and prepare for eventualities, so you can mitigate these risks and become a successful investor or entrepreneur. Buffett understands this truth very well, and that it is part and parcel of the world of investing. Calculated risk, as opposed to just risk, involves a lot of research, study, preparation, planning, and organizing. For instance, if you suddenly resign from a job you have held for quite some time in order to suddenly jump into a business opportunity, this is a risk you are taking. Calculated risk, however, weighs all the pros and cons, studies possible scenarios, researches the requirements and looks at how to best go about with this decision to start a venture.

Risk means putting your money into a company that you have

absolutely no idea about. On the other hand, calculated risk looks at the financial standing of the company, what the price to earnings ratio is, who is running the company behind the scenes, what the market looks like, and other factors to determine if investing in the company would be worth it. Buffett has been largely successful because of careful study and due diligence done prior to any investment decisions.

Lesson #3

"What the wise do in the beginning, fools do in the end."

This Buffett quote underscores the importance of research and laying the proper groundwork before making any major decisions, especially when it relates to financial investments. While Buffett has always had an understanding of business and wealth management, he does not neglect the intrinsic importance of scouting out the likely scenarios, preparing for eventualities, and having a structured roadmap towards the goal, rather than relying on a vague path that is more likely to miss than to hit.

What sets apart the smart, successful investors and business people from the mediocre ones is the amount of preparation that goes into each decision, from the smaller details to the larger acquisitions and mergers. Smart investors and entrepreneurs realize the value of a solid foundation that is backed up by careful study and well-researched data, especially in the volatile and ever-shifting business world. Research that is done towards the end of the process does not protect you from pitfalls and mistakes which may appear at the beginning stages. The wisest investors, like Buffett, know that the study must be done when the process is in its infancy.

Lesson #4

"The difference between successful people and very successful people is that very successful people say 'no' to almost everything."

When you look at the subsidiaries and assets of Warren Buffett, particularly his holdings in the Berkshire Hathaway conglomerate, you may think that he jumps at the chance to invest in almost anything as long as the price is right, or the opportunity is there. The opposite is true, however, as Buffett is actually quite finicky when it comes to which companies he would like to invest in. He knows when to say 'no', and more often than not, his instinct says 'no'.

This is an important lesson for anyone to remember regardless of his or her profession or calling in life. Just because an opportunity presents itself, or an offer is tendered to you, does not mean you should readily jump into it without knowing first what the likely consequences are, or if it is even the right fit for your short-term goals and long-term vision. Saying 'no' to a tempting offer can be difficult, especially if there are lucrative benefits on the surface which may obscure the larger problems or effects underneath.

Lesson #5

"Whether we are talking about socks or stocks, I like buying quality merchandise when it is marked down."

Buffett has made himself a well-regarded investor because he has the knack for finding himself at the right opportunity to purchase or invest into a company when it is at a better price. There is, in fact, quite a lot of common sense in this quote. If you can purchase something, whether it is a piece of clothing or a publicly traded stock, at a more affordable price without having to sacrifice quality, why not do it?

In many ways, quality is relative to price, of course. When a product is cheaper than most competitors, you may find that there is less it offers, or the quality is not as good. But there are also opportunities to buy top quality items at much lower prices, such as during clearance sales or seasonal promotions, so the enterprising, resourceful person can usually take advantage and get more bang per buck.

Lesson #6

"It's far better to buy a wonderful company at a fair price than a fair company at a wonderful price."

If you ask Buffett, he would rather invest in a company that has better reputation, earnings, potential, or trajectory at a fair price (meaning what its normal asking price would be) rather than a lesser-performing company at a much lower price. In this philosophy, Buffett is emphasizing quality and the importance of investing only in an opportunity that will enhance your portfolio and raise your standard, rather than settling for something less just because it is priced better. Have you ever found yourself settling for a lesser-quality product or service because it had a lower asking price than another competitor, only to find out later on that because it was inferior in durability or value, you actually ended up paying more than if you had just opted for the more expensive one in the first place? This can also be applied to business and investments, and Buffett is emphasizing that value, rather than price, should be the main determining factor for weighing a potential business or investment opportunity.

Lesson #7

"Price is what you pay. Value is what you get."

In this nugget of wisdom, Buffett is emphasizing that beyond the monetary cost of any commodity, stock, or product you are purchasing or investing in, there is a more intricate and long-lasting factor that lingers, and that is value. Value is the overall experience, usefulness, and effect of anything that you acquire, and far too many people are focused only on the immediate cost without considering the actual value in the long run.

There are plenty of cheap, low-cost options in the smartphone market, for instance. Models in the low-end market are coming out very frequently, all aimed at replicating the features of the more expensive brands and models and providing almost the same experience. But why are many people still willing to shell out hundreds of dollars more for the more expensive and established smartphone models and brands? It is because of the value that they get, the overall experience that comes with owning and using that phone, and how their past experience with the brand has made them realize how it interlaces with their daily lifestyle.

This is not to say, of course, that a lower price automatically means lower quality, as Buffett himself has advocated waiting for just the right opportunity to invest in an otherwise strategically positioned company that sees its market value decrease because of challenging factors. Markdowns certainly happen even for good buys, and this often does little to affect their quality. But Buffett knows that sometimes, you will have to decide to opt for a purchase that may cost a bit more, but deliver more returns over time, rather than go for the more inexpensive option with little rewards later on.

Lesson #8

"It is not necessary to do extraordinary things to get extraordinary results."

Early on life, Buffett already realized the value of hard work, strategic positioning, and figuring out what the market needs. From his early ventures in newspaper delivery and selling small food items, to setting up pinball machines in high-traffic areas such as barbershops, he discovered that it really does not require a grandiose scheme to earn money and reap the rewards. Sometimes, just a bit of common sense and timing can do the trick.

A lot of people have the notion that they need to know everything there is to know first about business, finance, and investments before they can jump in and actually start getting involved. To a certain extent, of course, planning and preparation are very important, but waiting until you understand every trick in the trade or figure out how each step of the process works can be disadvantageous, causing you to miss out on opportunities you could have grabbed already. Knowledge is important, but it is impossible to know everything, especially in the world of investing where most of the valuable lessons are learned while you are already in the thick of things.

Look for gaps in the market that need to be filled, or seasonal periods that require your expertise or commodity, and do what is necessary to deliver results. The small, often mundane-looking routines are actually the ones that deliver consistent results over time, as Buffett has proven in his successful investment strategies. Do not wait until you are some investment guru or financial whiz before heading out to the deep. The time to act may be now, and if you wait too long, the moment will pass.

Lesson #9

"The investor of today does not profit from yesterday's growth."

Successful investors and business people such as Buffett do not rest on their laurels. As soon as they have achieved something, they move on to the next challenge, looking for the next milestone to pass. Buffett knows that there are more frontiers to explore, more territories to conquer, so what he achieved yesterday is not enough.

In the world of business and entrepreneurship, successful people realize that while there is nothing wrong with celebrating your past success, there is also the tendency to become complacent and simply ride the wave of a past achievement. This can be very dangerous for the enterprise or venture. Simply riding the wave or coasting along can cause problems to be overlooked, mistakes left unchecked, and other small but significant errors compounding themselves into bigger obstacles later on.

If your goal is to become successful in your chosen career or venture, you should not allow yourself to rest on past platitudes. Rather, always challenge yourself to aim for something bigger, better, and higher. After you have overcome a challenge or achieved a goal, find the next one to aim for. Yesterday's success may not mean much tomorrow; just ask any of the big-name investors who incurred big losses during the 2007 financial crisis and were left with a shadow of what they were worth before the hit. The lesson is to keep pushing yourself to the limit, knowing that the future is uncertain.

Lesson #10

"Never invest in a business you cannot understand."

What is the point of trying to pour your energy, skills, resources, and time into a business venture or enterprise which, at its very core, you do not understand in the first place? This will lead to boredom, monotony, or a failure to identify what is needed to make the business grow, mostly because you do not even know what it is really all about. Passion is very important for anyone to have regarding a project or undertaking that they want to start. If your passion is the creative arts, you will find much joy and fulfilment in a profession that allows you to explore your imaginative side and pour your talent into expressions and creative output. However, if you force yourself into a highly technical or structured profession, eventually you will become restless and dissatisfied, and this will show in the work that you do as well.

In business, find an opportunity that is close to your interests and skills, or at least one that you can learn and appreciate, rather than a venture that is completely foreign to your understanding. After all, a successful business requires the leader to understand the workings of the machinery, and an appreciation for the ins and outs of the process. Otherwise, you will feel lost and overwhelmed, and this will spill over to your venture as well.

Lesson #11

"Rule Number 1: Never lose money. Rule Number 2: Never forget Rule Number 1."

A look at Buffett's various investment decisions will undoubtedly reveal that he himself has broken this rule quite a few times, particularly during the 2007-2008 financial crisis when his firm, Berkshire Hathaway, took massive losses. But in this popular Buffett quote, he is referring to the perspective or the mindset of an investor who eschews frivolous decision-making, excessive impulse-buying, and the lack of sensible analysis before making an all-important financial decision. When Buffett says to never lose money, he means that as an investor, entrepreneur, or business owner, you need to do your homework, complete your research, and study the situation before making a move. A wise investor does not enter into a deal or transaction with the attitude that it is alright to lose or take a hit because there is enough cushion to soften the fall. As an investor, Buffett highly values the importance of knowing the companies he wants to invest in, researching their positions and financial standings before making his decision. He is reminding you, as the investor, to avoid investing in a losing position.

Successful investors often have to avoid the bandwagon, going against the crowd or bucking the trend in order to carry something out. A wise person does not base his decision on what the rest of the crowd is doing, but rather on whether this decision will be favorable to his long-term goals and visions, regardless of what everyone else thinks.

Lesson #12

"Our favorite holding period is forever."

Buffett has been quoted as saying that if you are not very comfortable owning a particular company's stock for ten years, then you should not even be owning it for ten minutes. What does this mean? Buffett has been known to loyally hold on to most of the assets or stocks on his diversified portfolio even during times when the prices are down, or crises are causing a downturn, because he knows that eventually, things will turn around and he will benefit. On the other hand, Buffett is also underscoring the need to avoid investing in stocks that you would not want in your corner for very long, because more likely than not, this is coming from a short-sighted perspective.

An extended holding period acts as a buffer, or a way for an investor to refrain from making impulsive decisions, such as panicking right away, or being tempted by greed to immediately sell stocks when prices see a sudden decrease. These impulsive decisions have a negative effect on long-term portfolio appreciation. Unless a company has become obsolete or irrelevant, or is reeling from a drastic change that it likely cannot recover from, a long holding period, according to Buffett, is more beneficial especially if you are looking at a long-term portfolio.

Lesson #13

"I try to buy stock in businesses that are so wonderful, an idiot can run them. Sooner or later, one will."

What did Buffett mean when he said this? In the world of investment, you are always on the lookout for a company that would be a great buy, or going through a transition period that will leave it vulnerable or exposed, then stepping in when the time is right. In this quote, Buffett may be referring to identifying companies that have solid fundamentals, reliable foundations, and a well-oiled machinery that will continue to produce strong results even when changes take place, or leadership is handed over to new people.

But he could also be saying this from an opportunistic perspective. When someone who is relatively new, inexperienced, or foolish takes the helm of a company, it leaves that organization much more open to mistakes or failures caused by the new leader's wrong decisions, and you, as the investor, may be able to seize this chance to takeover and acquire a company you know you are capable of running. In a more practical sense, look at investing in firms that have already proven to be fundamentally sound and able to withstand human error and mistakes in judgment, because these companies are more likely to remain standing even when helmed by those with little experience or expertise to get behind the wheel. Investors should stay away from the cult of personality, focusing instead on how the organization functions as a whole, on its own.

Lesson #14

"Investors should remember that excitement and expenses are their enemies."

Buffett gave out this word of wisdom in a 2004 letter to shareholders, where he also talked about how an investor should be fearful when others are becoming greedy, or greedy when the rest of the market is cautious. When the market is full of investors who are excited about a particular stock or venture, prices go up due to the heightened demand. What happens is you will likely end up paying more for something that could very well be overhyped. On the other hand, being aggressive when other investors are holding on to their money often means chancing upon deals that are better-priced due to low demand, or catching opportunities when others are looking elsewhere.

This again underscores the importance of constant research, and of making decisions not based solely on stock market moods or investor bandwagons, but rather on solid fundamentals and a deep understanding of what works best for you and your venture, regardless of external factors. An experienced investor knows fully well that timing is everything, and there are many instances when gut instinct will dictate that he keeps still when others are moving aggressively, or that he move quickly when others are choosing to hit the brakes. Buffett has found much success in this philosophy, placing him in positions of big returns because he did not let the market's cautious mood derail him from seizing what he knew would be advantageous for his holdings.

Lesson #15

"You don't have to swing at everything."

Patience is a necessary component of successful investing and financial management. There will be plenty of offers, opportunities, and seemingly good deals thrown your way all the time, but just like in baseball, you can wait patiently for your pitch rather than listening to all the fans screaming at you to swing. Buffett has referred to the stock market as a "no-called-strike" game. You can take your time and wait for the right opportunity.

Buffett has often said that his first experience with stocks, as an eleven-year-old owning and later on selling shares of Cities

Service Preferred, taught him the value of being patient as an investor. When the shares rose to $40 (from his purchase price of $38), he sold the shares at a small profit, but later regretted the decision when Cities Service shares actually reached $200 each.

The reality, however, is that patience is a lesson that all investors, business entrepreneurs, and financial professionals must learn on their own through their various experiences. It is part of the learning process, and must be seen first-hand in order to build character and leave an indelible mark. Just remember not to take a swing at everything that comes your way, because a better opportunity could be waiting around the corner. Strategically position and time your moves, knowing that each decision has an effect on the future.

Lesson #16

"Fear is the foe of the faddist, but the friend of the fundamentalist."

Buffett gave this nugget of advice in a 1994 Chairman's Letter sent out to his firm. He was actually referring to his company's general direction of continuing to disregard whatever forecasts or predictions were being given regarding the political or socioeconomic situations around the world. The investment mogul cited, as an example, how just a few decades prior to 1994, experts could not have predicted how the Vietnam War broke out and protracted into a years-long conflict, how wage regulation and price controls were imposed, the sudden rise and fall of oil prices and the massive changes in the oil industry, the fall of the Soviet Union, or even the steep one-day decline in the Dow Jones. However, as Buffett pointed out, these massive events had little effect on the investment foundations of his mentor Benjamin Graham's holdings, particularly because his investment decisions were based not on the shock factor or knee-jerk reactions of social events, but on sounds business principles.

In this lesson, Buffett is saying that no matter what the global climate may be, if you are to continue as a financial investor, you should stick to the essentials of the practice and not let the fear of the unknown or the uncertainty of the times take over. Indeed, the global economy goes through upswings and downturns, but everything comes to pass, and decisions should not be based on apprehensions or worries, but on what has been proven to be effective for long-term yields.

Lesson #17

"The truly big investment idea can usually be explained in a short paragraph."

Buffett also mentioned this statement in his 1994 Chairman's Letter, underscoring why his firm continues to believe in carrying on investments that are fewer in number and simpler in concept. After all, as he says in the letter, the degree of an investment's difficulty does not count, nor do you get any additional perks or bonus points for coming up with the more complicated investments. Rather, it is the returns that speak volumes and that truly matter in the end.

Buffett has constantly showed that he goes for businesses with enduring competitive edge (for instance, those in the insurance and pre-need industries) and managed by leaders who are people-oriented. When these characteristics are combined with sensible costs and strong business fundamentals, risks are lowered, and the situation is less prone to volatility. On the other hand, investment opportunities that are unreasonably complicated, bogged down by shifting variables and complex systems, do not necessarily mean profits anyway, so why overburden yourself? Go for opportunities that are easy to figure out and with enduring, proven strategies.

Lesson #18

"It's the lack of change that appeals to me ... that's the kind of business I like."

Buffett made this statement in 1999 referring to Wrigley Company, the American chewing gum company in which his firm, Berkshire Hathaway, had a minority equity investment until late 2016. Buffett, unlike many modern investors, saw the traditional business direction of Wrigley as its strength rather than its weakness, stating that he does not think that the Internet or its transformative power will hurt the business fundamentals of Wrigley.

Buffett also stated in the interview with BusinessWeek that his company's focus is to profit from a company's lack of directional change, rather than from change itself. In other words, he likes to identify those companies that are still going in the same direction and finding success in sticking to their foundations despite the ever-changing variables around them. He believes that companies who buck the trends can also be great investments, especially those whose primary market and services will remain the same despite the uncertainties around them.

Change in itself, of course, is not bad. Change can be positive, and allow an enterprise or organization to position itself more strategically and face the challenges of the future. However, there are also plenty of instances wherein change can actually be harmful to the health and vision of a venture, especially when the change is implemented only for the sake of going with the trend rather than as a precursor to expansion or advancement. While many in today's business climate like to champion the importance of change, Buffett is attracted more by those companies that are changing very little from how they were established.

Lesson #19

"Time is the friend of the wonderful business."

This is Buffett's take on the popular saying, "Only time will tell." Some of the biggest decisions that an investor or entrepreneur will make may not seem right at the moment, but only the future will reveal whether or not it was the correct decision. In some of Buffett's investments, for instance, his decision to transition Berkshire Hathaway from a textile manufacturing company into the multinational conglomerate it is today, the rewards were not immediate, and it took years for any fruits to actually show.

An investor must come to terms with the reality that some of his decisions will be misunderstood by those around him, even those closest to him. However, a wise investor is not just looking at the here and now, but has his eyes set on the bigger picture, and looking ahead often means having to conjure up the strength to look beyond any difficulties that lie in the immediate path.

In this letter to shareholders in 1989, Buffett also mentioned that time is an "enemy of the mediocre", which also holds much truth. To the average person, having to wait a little longer to see any gains or rewards is not worth it. The mediocre person prefers quick results, but the truly successful investors and entrepreneurs understand the value of trusting the process in its entirety. Successful people, just like Buffett, forego immediate gains, choosing instead to prioritize longevity, stability, and even bigger investment returns that only time will reveal.

Lesson #20

"In the business world, the rear-view mirror is always clearer than the windshield."

In this memorable Buffett quote, the rear-view mirror represents hindsight, or the analysis after the fact, while the windshield refers to what is in front of you at the moment. What may seem very obvious or clear when presented to you is actually blurred or distorted compared to what you will see later on as you are looking back.

This fact can be either a positive encouragement or a negative disillusionment to an investor or entrepreneur. On the positive side, you can look at this as a challenge to always aim for bigger and better things, knowing that you will really only see the full picture once everything is said and done. But you may also take this negatively and err too much on the cautious side because the road ahead is uncertain, and not everything is clear to see right away.

How do you apply this Buffet advice to your daily life? Self-assessment is key to improving your knowledge and acumen as an investor or business person, so looking at the rear-view mirror and analyzing what you did right, what you did wrong, and what you could have done better must be part of the equation. Because hindsight is a more accurate barometer of success or failure, do not be afraid to look back and measure how well you did on that past challenge. This strengthens your resolve, improves your efficiency, and makes you better equipped to handle similar situations in the future, should you find yourself in that predicament once again.

These are some of the most well-known quotes about investing that have been attributed to Warren Buffett. But what does the great business magnate and investment legend have to say about people and relationships in general? In the next chapter, let us look at some of his philosophies and insights regarding interpersonal relationships.

Lessons Summary

- Warren Buffett likes to wait in the wings for a company that is going through a difficult time, then pounce in on the investment opportunity.
- In business and investment, Buffett understands that risk is part of the process, but mostly stems from not knowing what to do. Calculated risk can minimize risks and mitigate losses.
- Buffett also emphasizes the need for due diligence, scoping out the scenarios and understanding the realities of an opportunity before investing.
- Investors must learn to say 'no' to offers more than they say 'yes', at least according to Buffett.
- Buffett likes a good bargain, especially when it is a top-quality company stock or acquisition that has been marked down.
- However, Buffett also points out that he would rather acquire a high-performing company at market price than shell out less money for an underperformer.
- Buffett also realizes that value, more than just price, should be factored into the decision-making regarding an investment.
- According to Buffett, you often do not need to be the most extraordinary person in your field to be able to achieve outstanding results.
- Successful investors keep on looking for the next challenges and rarely ever become content with what they have already achieved.
- Buffett also advocates investing in a business opportunity you actually understand and

appreciate, rather than a venture you have not even begun to fathom.

- One of Buffett's most famous quotes, "Never lose money", refers to strategic planning and research before making any major financial decisions.
- Also, Buffett says unless you are prepared to have an asset or stock for a long time, don't bother adding it to your portfolio.
- Buffett says you should look for companies that can stand on their own and deliver results, even when transition happens and poor leadership takes over.
- According to Buffett, you should be cautious when others are excited, and aggressive when other investors are being overly careful.
- He also cautions against taking a shot at every opportunity, focusing instead on timing and precision.
- Buffett dislikes overly complicated investment ideas, favoring the simple, easily understood proposals instead.
- He leans towards businesses that have undergone little change, saying these are the ones that are often more stable.
- Buffett underscores the reality that time is often the real barometer of success. Many results do not happen right away.

Chapter Two: Warren's Words On Human Relationships

Warren Buffett is the master when it comes to finance and investments, but he also has a lot of wisdom to impart regarding interpersonal relationships. Here are some of his most memorable quotes about human relationships, interactions, friendships and what we can learn from them:

Lesson #21

"A very rich person should leave his kids enough to do anything, but not enough to do nothing."

Buffett has three children from his first marriage, and while they have grown up in privilege and wealth unlike many of their peers, Buffett also made sure they understood the value of work ethic and labor. In this quote, Buffett reminds investors who have found some level of financial success that there is nothing wrong with leaving behind a legacy of wealth to their children, but that the importance of hard work should still be imparted to the next generation.

It has been said that among the rich families, family wealth significantly declines after the first generation due to mismanagement, poor decisions, or neglect. This occurs when wealthy parents do not leave behind important lessons on management and patience to their children. Instead of just wealth, a wealthy investor should endeavor to set his children on the path towards finding their own success in the world, instead of just relying on a trust fund or credit line that will vanish if not properly managed.

Lesson #22

"Someone is sitting in the shade today because someone else planted a tree a long time ago."

This Buffett quote can be interpreted as referring to the long, protracted process of investing and reaping its rewards, but it may also refer to the value of learning from the experiences of others that have gone before you, and the foundations that have been laid out by those whose efforts have contributed to where you stand today in the industry.

No matter what industry, profession, or career you are involved in today, there are others before you who have paved the way and who have experienced their own ups and downs, and their anecdotes or words of wisdom will be of value to you as you forge your own path. This could be a family member, a friend, a colleague, or other acquaintance who can guide you towards the right direction.

Lesson #23

"You can't make a good deal with a bad person."

Because of the size of Berkshire Hathaway and the influence of Buffett in business matters, many investors, business owners, and entrepreneurs regularly meet with him and his managers, seeking opportunities for partnerships. In this statement, Buffett emphasizes that even the most carefully studied business deal with sound principles and proper preparation cannot make up for the mistake of ending up in a deal with a bad person.

Buffett has always said that there is much more to the world of investing than just looking at business principles and trajectories, although these are certainly very important. Of greater weight to the successful investor is the character, reputation, and integrity of the person or group he will be going into business with, so beyond just the variables, he wants to look at the track record of the people behind the business.

What lesson can you pick up from this statement? No matter how tempting or lucrative an offer may look like, if it will potentially put you on the same side of things as suspicious characters with dubious track records, it is best to steer clear and to look for other partnerships with those who have unquestionable integrity. In the long run, this will turn out to be a better business decision and will far outweigh any immediate financial windfall.

Lesson #24

"It takes 20 years to build a reputation, and five minutes to ruin it."

Buffett may choose to work only with people of unparalleled character and integrity as much as possible, but he also sets a high standard for himself in his dealings. In this statement,

Buffett reminds investors and entrepreneurs that it is very important to safeguard their reputation and practice caution in personal and professional dealings, because a misstep can render years of hard work and perseverance useless, especially in this age of information and fast communication. Even the most secretive or privacy-committed entrepreneurs or investors will find themselves under the spotlight, being closely scrutinized by the public. This is because in the business community, many see a potential partner's personal life as an indication of their trustworthiness, dependability, and character. After all, if someone cannot be trusted with matters regarding their personal life, why would you entrust financial or entrepreneurial decisions to them?

As a leader, investor, or business entrepreneur, you should always remind yourself to treat your position with the utmost responsibility and caution, and avoid situations that may lead to questionable behavior, actions, or misconceptions. The same respect and dignity you afford yourself and your position in the industry will also be given to you by your peers and colleagues, and this will enable you to maximize opportunities presented by those who wish to have dealings with you.

Lesson #25

"It's better to hang out with people better than you."

The company you keep will have a huge impact on the kind of person you turn out to be, the decisions that you make, your interests and experiences, and even your perspectives on the industry or life in general. As such, it is important that you choose friends who are positive, encouraging, and enriching to your personal and professional life, rather than acquaintances who pull you down and make you focus on the negative things.

Buffett reminds us in this quote that friendships and acquaintances tend to rub off their attitudes, opinions, and behaviors on us. Are you choosing to spend time with people who have an optimistic view of life and want to seek out the advancement of the community at large? Or are you spending your free time with those who are focused only on personal gain without much regard to any contribution to the society? It has been said that one of Buffett's closest friends is Microsoft owner Bill Gates, with whom he plays bridge every week. Their friendship has blossomed from a casual relationship into a concerted desire to leave an indelible mark on the world, as they have partnered in efforts to give away much of their wealth to charitable causes around the world. In this effort, they have also inspired other big names in business, finance, and investment to share more of their personal wealth towards projects and causes that help humanity.

Lesson #26

"You will move in the direction of the people that you associate with."

Closely related to the previous statement, Buffett said this to a group of students who listened to one of his speeches at Columbia University. Interestingly, another person who shared the stage with him at the lecture was his good friend Gates. According to Buffett, the right group of friends can challenge you to achieve much bigger goals in your professional life, and can provide you with the right mental and emotional support to push yourself to limits you may not have thought you could reach.

Another advantage of good, enriching friends is the opportunity to widen your network and be introduced to contacts who can inspire, invigorate, and open up your life to different possibilities. As you build your network of contacts, you may even find potential business partners or entrepreneurs who have access to products, services, or ideas you will deem necessary in future expansion plans.

No man is an island, as it is often said. Since our normal human tendency is to reach out and make friends, make these friendships count, choosing enriching relationships and challenging connections that encourage you to become a better version of yourself, always aimed at personal advancement.

Lesson #27

"Of the billionaires I have known, money just brings out the basic traits in them."

In this statement, Buffett points out that wealth in itself is a neutral commodity, meaning it does not make someone a better or worse person. Rather, it only compounds or highlights those traits or characteristics that were already present in that person before he reached that level of financial success. Very telling indeed, coming from someone who has attained such success in finance and investments, and therefore has met so many rich, powerful, and moneyed individuals throughout his life.

Buffett goes on to say that if a person was already a mean-spirited individual before becoming rich, their behavior now tends to still be mean-spirited and ill-willed, only now he has the wealth to make him more entitled, abusive, or insensitive towards others. On the opposite end of the spectrum, someone who was raised to be compassionate, caring, and sensitive to the needs and feelings of people around him will likely still display these traits even after becoming very wealthy. In fact, their wealth will likely enable them to reach out to those in need and become a conduit of compassion. Are you finding yourself changing for the better as you attain more success financially, or are you noticing negative traits or characteristics, perhaps pointed out by other people around you? Instead of blaming it on the financial status, which in itself is a neutral factor, you should focus instead on developing positive and compassionate habits incorporated into your lifestyle, keeping you grounded and level-headed, and with the constant reminder that wealth and status are not all that there is to life. How you deal with people around you is what matters more.

Lesson #28

"The obligation of a society as prosperous as ours is to figure out how nobody gets left too far behind."

In terms of philanthropy and charitable giving, Buffett lives out this very principle, donating billions of dollars of his personal wealth to various charitable organizations, such as the Bill and Melinda Gates Foundation, the Nuclear Threat Initiative, Girls, Inc., Glide Foundation, and the Buffett Foundation.

In 2010, it was reported that Buffett, his friend Gates, and Facebook's CEO Mark Zuckerberg signed an agreement which was dubbed the Gates-Buffett Giving Pledge. In this campaign, the three billionaires promised to give away the majority of their wealth to various philanthropic and charitable causes. The campaign spread among billionaires and millionaires, and as of 2017, the Giving Pledge already has 158 signers. Pledges have accumulated to over $365 billion.

According to Buffett, "The Giving Pledge is about asking wealthy families to have important conversations about their wealth and how it will be used."

Prior to the Giving Pledge, Buffett had already pledged over 99% of his wealth to the Gates Foundation. This includes a pledge of 10 million Class B shares of Berkshire Hathaway pledged to the said foundation, with about 5% of the donation being received by the organization each year.

What can you take away from this initiative started by Buffett? There are many worthy causes in your community or neighborhood that would benefit from your charitable giving, and if you find that you have been financially blessed because of your investments, business ventures, enterprises, and other income sources, one of your priorities should be to help out in whatever way you can towards the alleviation of societal problems. Buffett and the other wealthy investors and entrepreneurs involved in philanthro-capitalism have realized that when they give towards the less fortunate sectors of society, they are also making an investment in a better future, and leaving an indelible mark that would change the lives of generations to come.

What you will find as you become more active in business and investments is that there is little fulfilment to be achieved when you focus only on yourself. Yes, you may find the pleasures of life enjoyable for a time, but after taking it all in, soon you will realize the emptiness of a life that is lived only toward oneself. On the other hand, those who have discovered the joy of living for others, such as Buffett, can attest to the incredibly fulfilling, satisfying, and enriching experience that comes from knowing that you are instrumental in impacting lives and communities for decades to come.

Lesson #29

"If you get to my age in life and nobody thinks well of you, I do not care how big your bank account is. Your life is a disaster."

Today's materialistic society is focused on making money and achieving success in career, business, or other endeavors. It is not wrong to aim for success in life, or to try to achieve financial stability and independence. But if it is all that you are living for, and you neglect the more important thing, which is to become a beacon of hope, encouragement, and compassion in your circle of influence, it becomes empty and meaningless towards the end of your life.

Buffett realized this in his storied career which is why he has taken significant steps to create considerable positive impact on the world using his wealth.

At the same time, he knows that it is far more important to leave a legacy of compassion, generosity, and influence rather than to be known only as someone who may have amassed riches but did not contribute anything significant to the plight of others.

Have you ever assessed your life and thought about what others will think of you when you pass on? Sure, you may be focused on growing your business or creating an entrepreneurial empire, or finding the most lucrative investments for the most yields in the future, but think about it: will all of this really matter when you leave this earth and those you will leave behind will talk about your impact on their lives? Again, it is not wrong to amass wealth or to achieve success in life, but any notable achievements in these areas will only become truly meaningful when they are used to touch the lives of your family, loved ones, friends, and community.

Lesson #30

"Honesty is a very expensive gift. Don't expect it from cheap people."

Buffett realized early in life that not all the people he would come across would be authentic, genuine, or trustworthy. Many are there because they have a personal agenda or would see him as a means to an end. Some are there because they want to take what they can get, or somehow ride his coattails to success. Some are stealing his ideas or copying his moves, attempting to replicate his strategies for success. This is why Buffett referred to honesty in interpersonal relationships as an expensive gift; not very many people can afford to truly give it all the time.

Take a moment to stop and think about your relationships, and how much honesty you are really getting. How often do you get authentic, uncensored, truly constructive critiques from those you consider to be friends or colleagues? If all you are getting is one side of the picture, that is not honesty at all. Honesty means being able to get both positive and negative remarks that are meant to build you up and make you a better person.

Remember, if your friends can lie or gossip to you about other people in your circle, chances are they are also doing the same thing to you behind your back. Successful investors know full well that they will have to dissociate themselves from people who are dishonest, manipulative, deceitful, or like to sow discord. Buffett, in this quote, compares honesty and authentic relationships to a costly investment. If your friends truly care about you as a person, they will not hesitate to invest in your betterment through honest and frank discussions.

Lesson #31

"Having first-rate people on the team is more important than designing hierarchies and clarifying who reports to whom."

According to Buffett, the attitude, integrity, reliability, and work ethic of people whom you will be partnering or working with should be prioritized over and above the meticulous structuring of the organizational flow chart, or obsessive attention to job titles and positions. Yes, it is important to clearly hash out the details regarding what each team member is expected to do, what their individual responsibilities are, and what each position contributes to the team as a whole. But more than job titles, leaders and entrepreneurs should look at the level of commitment of a potential staff member or business partner.

Buffett places a premium on hiring individuals who are honest, passionate workers, and with the intelligence and creativity to boot, because these qualities are of more importance than spending too much time organizing the hierarchical structure of the team, or figuring out who should lead and who should follow. In other words, if you are working with genuine team members, it will not matter much to them whether the organizational roles are being meticulously followed. In a healthy working environment, job titles take a backseat to group efforts and team players.

Again, this is not to assume that job titles and positions are no longer important, but only to point out that for successful investors, intuitive and careful selection of partners and team members often lead them to working with individuals who care far more about getting the job done rather than spending an inordinate amount of time wondering who should do it. It is a mark of maturity, intelligence, and commitment to success.

Lesson #32

"If you hire somebody without integrity, you really want them to be dumb and lazy."

The hiring process is one of the most crucial components of the entrepreneurial process, especially if you are just starting out and are directly involved in selecting who your team members will be. Buffett believes that a potential hire should have intelligence, energy, and integrity, but of the three qualities, it is integrity that should stand out.

Why would hiring someone without the virtue of integrity or trustworthiness make that person lazy? Hiring someone who is smart and passionate but with questionable character will make that person believe that he can get by in life just because he has the brains and the brawn, and he will not see the need to also develop the best asset of all: character beyond reproach.

Lesson #33

"If each of us hires people who are bigger than we are, we shall become a company of giants."

Another word of advice that Buffett dishes out regarding the selection of people to work with is to choose people who are better, stronger, faster, more intuitive, more creative, or more experienced than you perceive yourself to be. Many business owners and entrepreneurs are intimidated by the notion of someone on their team presumably having more skills and experience than they do, but think of it this way: if you have that person on your team, that is an advantage for your company.

An investor or entrepreneur with a top-quality team will have more chances of churning out top-tier results and staying ahead of the competition, so do not be afraid of luring the best and the brightest talent out there and inviting them to your corner. Again, a mature investor or business owner will know that each person on his team will contribute skills, ideas, experiences, and passion that will raise the company's standard for excellence and allow the organization to achieve greater heights.

If you want to be mediocre in your efforts, then choose to work with mediocre, average people. But if you really desire to go beyond expectations, the people on your team are just as important as the peers or friends you associate yourself with. Make hiring selections that will challenge you and cause your venture to become a dream team, rather than an amateur selection that caters to your ego.

These are some of the popular quotes attributed to Warren Buffett revealing his thoughts and insights regarding people and relationships. In the next chapter, let us look at

---

memorable statements that Buffett has said regarding personal development and learning, and how you can constantly make yourself a better professional, investor, entrepreneur, or career person.

Lessons Summary

- Warren Buffett has publicly stated that his children will not inherit a large fortune from his wealth, but rather, they have been trained to stand on their own two feet and achieve financial independence.
- Buffett understands the importance of looking back and appreciating the contributions that others before you have made to your current path or industry, and learning from them in any way you can.
- Even the best business deal, if made with a person of bad reputation or questionable integrity, will not yield positive results, says Buffett.
- Buffett reminds investors and leaders that a few minutes of uncontrolled emotions, actions, or words can erode any positive influence or reputation built over the years, so each action or word must be carefully weighed.
- Buffett believes in associating with people who are challenging, enriching, and more intelligent, because eventually these qualities will make you a better individual.
- According to Buffett, people who are innately good-hearted and who become financially successful will use their wealth towards good causes, while those who are self-centered and greedy from the start will change very little once they become rich. Because of this, a good and moral foundation in life is necessary.

- Buffett has enlisted the help of many of his wealthy friends in making billions of dollars' worth of pledges towards charitable causes worldwide, because he believes it is his responsibility to impact this world in a good way using his resources.
- Also, Buffett believes that way beyond any material possessions or accolades, how you are viewed by the people around you, and the kind of legacy you pass on to your sphere of influence, has greater weight when all is said and done.
- Honesty, says Buffett, can only be given to you by genuine friends and kin who truly care about you. Honest opinions are just as much of an investment, so you should also invest in good friendships and relationships.
- When it comes to hiring or partnerships, Buffett says it is more important to look at a person's integrity rather than his talents or skills. Also, if you can, work with people who are better than you.

Chapter Three: Buffett's Advice for Betterment

I imagine the very reason why you have read through this book on the words of wisdom from Warren Buffett is because you are genuinely interested in becoming a better investor, entrepreneur, manager, leader, business owner, or professional. There is so much to learn from the experiences and advice of others, or from those who have proven themselves as leaders and forerunners in their respective fields of expertise.

Warren Buffett has also made many pronouncements and statements regarding how you can become better at what you do. How you can develop the skills and talents you already have, build on your current knowledge, expand your capabilities, and increase your marketability in an ever-changing business climate. Here are some of his sagely words:

Lesson #34

"Predicting rain does not count. Building arks does."

In an obvious reference to the Biblical story of Noah's ark and the great flood, Buffett differentiates between predictions and planning. In this quote, he refers to the reality that having a keen sense of awareness regarding possible scenarios or coming circumstances does little to make you a better investor, entrepreneur, or leader. Rather, it is how you plan, prepare, and take control of your situation that truly defines whether you will become successful in your endeavors. What difference does it make if you are always monitoring market trends, stock prices, company earnings, or business forecasts when you do very little to hedge your entity or venture against upheavals and changes. In the story of Noah, when he was made aware of the coming deluge, not only did he warn about the impending destruction, but he also followed orders to build a massive sea vessel that would protect his family and the animal species that would be boarded onto the ark. In the end, him and his family, along with the animals, were saved from the great flood because he was adequately prepared, with supplies aboard the ark that enabled them to survive for weeks while the earth was submerged.

Forecasts and trends should be used not only for knowledge, but also for taking the appropriate action. Use the knowledge made available to you to strengthen your holdings, improve your financial standing, and make the necessary steps to prepare for eventualities. This is what really counts. On the other hand, knowledge that does not spur you into action is useless and cannot protect you from what may happen in the future.

Lesson #35

"What we learn from history is that people do not learn from history."

Past experiences should be building blocks to better decision making, more enlightened choices, and improved efficiency and management for the investor, entrepreneur, or leader. Buffett emphasizes in this lesson that history tends to repeat itself, and the wise ones will see this trend and avoid making the same mistakes over and over again. On the other hand, those who have not learned from the past are bound to make the same errors yet again.

As you assess your decisions, identify areas that were unsuccessful, and make an honest analysis of what could be done right the next time the situation presents itself. Are there steps that should not have been neglected, or transactions that should be avoided so as not to repeat the errors? Should the advice of peers or insiders be heeded the next time, or should you go with what your gut instinct told you? Are there other personnel who are better equipped to handle the tasks next time, or is it better to outsource to other professionals outside your organization for better results? All of these factors should be taken into account, and combined towards a more informed decision that will hopefully allow you to achieve a better outcome the next time.

Mistakes are bound to happen, especially in the world of business and investments. But your strength and success as a leader will shine through if you are able to avoid replicating failures that otherwise could be averted through proper planning and adjustment of strategies and methods. While a failure is often unavoidable, it is inexcusable to fall into the same downward path numerous times especially when a solution can be worked out. Learn from your past missteps, and you come out a more efficient leader.

It may often require asking the assistance of an outside

observer to look at your strategies and techniques. There is truth to the notion that the best coaches are sometimes those who are not in the game itself, simply because they have a different perspective when watching the game from afar rather than in the thick of things. Do not hesitate to seek the assistance of people who may be able to help you achieve the desired results through honest criticism.

Lesson #36

"Chains of habits are too light to be felt until they are too heavy to be broken."

This Buffett quote emphasizes the importance of developing good habits as an investor, entrepreneur, manager, or professional. The small decisions you make every day become habits over time, and if these habits are positive and enriching, they will help you to achieve your short-term and long-term goals. However, bad habits may also form, and these negative traits will hinder you from achieving your full potential, and what is more worrisome is the fact that so many times, they do not become apparent until they have reared their ugly heads and caused a big mess.

Take stock of your daily habits and lifestyle choices. Are you managing your time wisely from the time you get up in the morning until you retire at night? Or are there a lot of times during the day that are wasted on unnecessary activities that can be eliminated or simply rescheduled? Are you finding yourself procrastinating until the last minute, only to find yourself extremely stressed out and producing low quality work? This becomes a very bad habit that will have a negative impact on your effectivity as a leader.

Form habits that complement your long-term vision and allow you to reach, rather than get side-tracked from, what you want to achieve on a daily basis. When good habits are formed early on, they become an integral part of your lifestyle and will be hard to break. At the same time, identify those small bad habits, and seek to correct them right away, long before they become systemic and embedded in your psyche. As Buffett says in this quote, do not wait until they have become too heavy and more difficult to be free from.

Lesson #37

"Do not save what is left after spending, but spend what is left after saving."

Financial management requires you to always be looking at the bigger picture, or the possibilities that may occur in the future. Rather than rounding up whatever is left of your funds and putting that towards savings or emergency funds, prioritize the savings first, and then spend what is available. In business, this is also referred to as paying yourself first, because putting funds towards savings is considered as a self-payment.

Why does Buffett suggest this to investors and entrepreneurs? Prioritizing savings allows you to set aside a fixed amount that will help with the rainy days when cash flow is not as steady. On the other hand, simply releasing the funds for expenses and then waiting for anything left over to put towards a savings account will likely leave you with very little, and your cushion for emergencies will be substantially reduced. Savings should be prioritized, and then expenses adjusted accordingly after the savings has already been deducted from the income.

It may not seem like the most business-friendly step to take now, especially when you have overhead expenses, payroll, and other payments to think about. A wise investor or entrepreneur, however, realizes that cash flow in the business sector can often be volatile, and if he wants to stay in the game longer, he must have enough of a financial fall back to be able to weather any sudden downturns in the business climate.

Lesson #38

"I insist on a lot of time being spent, almost every day, to just sit and think."

Buffett acknowledges that this piece of advice is very uncommon today in the American business sector. People are too busy doing, travelling, meeting with staff or other potential business partners, running around completing errands and tasks, that there is just not a lot of time left over for sitting and thinking. In fact, many frown upon it as a waste of time.

But not Buffett, the successful investor who is running a billion-dollar conglomerate. He says he makes sure to take time each day to just sit, think, and read. This becomes his time to take stock of what he wants to do, where he is as far as his short-term and long-term goals, and also allows him to avoid knee-jerk reactions or impulsive decisions. Sudden reactions or hasty decisions are often the by-product of very little time for reflection and assessment. If you want to avoid more mistakes as you go along your career, place an importance on giving yourself ample time to just sit, relax, and think things over. This is not a waste of time.

Lesson #39

"I always knew I was going to be rich. I don't think I ever doubted it for a minute."

A look at Buffett's life, from his childhood on, reveals a person who, very early in his life, knew what he wanted to do and determined in his mind to pursue his passion. The battle really starts in the mind. If you think you can, then you can achieve great things. But if you are constantly doubting yourself or putting yourself down, or worse, comparing yourselves to others and playing up your weaknesses, it will not be surprising if you do not amount to much.

There is a lot of power in how you view yourself and your capabilities. If you have already won the struggle within you, there is very little that outside factors or voices can do to deter you from your goal. In the same way, no amount of outside motivation or opportunities will spur you into action if you do not believe in yourself and your potential first.

Are you listening to negativity and self-doubt, or are you winning the battle in your mind through enriching habits, encouraging words, and self-affirmation? Confidence should start within yourself, and this will reflect in your decisions, actions, words, and reactions. How you develop your self-esteem will also build your determination to succeed in the path you have chosen to take. Take control of your thoughts!

Lesson #40

"You need to fill your mind with various competing thoughts, and decide which make sense."

Buffett was a voracious reader since childhood, recounting how by the age of ten years old, he had already read every book on financial investments available in the public library of his hometown, Omaha. Because he started early, he developed his skills, fine-tuned his strategies, and found a lot of opportunities to test his knowledge.

What you fill your mind with becomes your passion. If your goal is to become a successful entrepreneur, set out to learn all there is to know about entrepreneurship by reading, researching, and networking with those who can impart knowledge to you. You cannot expect to become successful in the field of business and entrepreneurship if you are spending most of your day focused on other things. Passion demands that you invest time, energy, and effort into the path you are determined to conquer.

Becoming a successful person is not defined just by income or wealth, as Buffett has already realized. Rather, there is more fulfilment in discovering how you have grown as a person because of the experiences, knowledge, and challenges you have encountered in life. All of these will combine to elevate your status to the next level of excellence, and it starts with being open to knowledge and discovery.

Lesson #41

"A person's main asset is themselves, so preserve and enhance yourself."

Health, wellness, and fitness are very popular topics these days. People are placing an increased importance on being healthy, staying healthy, and finding ways to improve wellness in the midst of a stressful society. Buffett reminds investors, entrepreneurs, and leaders to take care of the body and the mind, because that is the only one they have. The mind, in particular, can be enhanced over time through learning, while the body should be preserved through good habits.

Buffett does not partake of alcohol or recreational drugs, although he does consume caffeine (particularly Coca-Cola). He has remained quite healthy for his age despite a stage I prostate cancer diagnosis in 2012, from which he has been able to recover.

Are you taking care of your physical, mental, and spiritual health, or are these taking a backseat in your quest to become successful in your field of endeavor? The sacrifices you take now regarding health and wellness will take their toll on you later in life, and will prevent you from enjoying the fruits of your labor. Instead of overworking yourself and neglecting health and wellness, strive to maintain a healthy balance now, and you will have ample time even as you get older to reap the rewards of success.

Set aside time for your body to relax, rejuvenate, and replenish itself. It is not advisable to so fill up your schedule and leave hardly enough time for personal relaxation, let alone exercise. If you are finding yourself having difficulty concentrating on tasks, or having a hard time maintaining focus or energy, this could be a sign that your body and mind are overworked, and need attention as well. According to Buffett, you should also invest in yourself, and in fact, it is your investment in yourself that should be the most substantial, because you are your greatest asset.

Lesson #42

"Read five hundred pages like this every day. That's how knowledge works."

Buffett still reads about five newspapers every day, aside from other publications, which is why he is knowledgeable about so many things and has managed to stay in the loop even though he is not as technologically-updated as his counterparts. He likens reading to compounded interest, because it builds up your knowledge over time.

There are plenty of ways for today's entrepreneur, leader, or investor to consume reading material. Aside from the printed page, many publications and books are now in digital format, available for computers, smartphones, and tablets. There are also books in audio format, allowing you to listen to a book while driving. There is no excuse, no matter how hectic your schedule may be, to remain uninformed in this time of free-flowing information.

The fact that you have taken the time to read through this book on Warren Buffett's memorable quotes is already a step in the right direction. There is plenty of reading material available today that will enhance your knowledge, teach valuable lessons, and give you a peek into the lives of the world's most successful leaders and trailblazers. If your goal is self-development, reading cannot be neglected.

Lesson #43

"The best thing I did was to choose the right heroes."

Who do you look up to as role models, mentors, or examples in your life? In his life, Buffett looked up to the investment magnate and author Benjamin Graham, who later turned out to be his college professor, mentor, and employer. When Graham retired and closed his firm, many of his successful tactics and strategies were replicated by Buffett in his own partnerships, and he became successful as well.

Buffett knew that if he wanted to find a pattern for success, he needed to look for examples of right decision making, strategic planning, and sound business principles. People look for role models in everything, whether it is in sports, education, entertainment, or any other area in life. Who you look up to will have a major impact on how you live your life, so it is important to choose them well.

Look for role models who are finding success in their respective professions or business ventures, and are looking for ways to give back to the community, impart their knowledge, and contribute to a better humanity. These role models will teach you the real value of a shared human experience, and expose you to the realities of today's globalized business climate where the more prosperous can no longer afford to ignore the plight of those left behind by progress.

Perhaps your role model is someone closer to home, such as a family member, colleague, or a hometown hero. Learn from them, connect with them personally, and share with them your aspirations, dreams, perspectives, and plans for the future. When you open up to another person who is wiser and more experienced, you are also receiving their wisdom and valuable insights, and this is often just as important, if not more effective, than any college course or business class you will attend. Real-life experiences, after all, are the best teachers, and when imparted by those who went through them can be highly efficient in getting the message across.

There is so much to learn about the world of business, finance, and investments, and if you have someone in your life who can personally guide you and mentor you, you are already on the right track. Warren Buffett credits much of his achievements to those who came before him and were unselfish in sharing what they know, imparting lifelong lessons he still treasures to this day. When the time comes, you may also have the chance to share what you know and recount your experiences to another aspiring leader, investor, or entrepreneur, so do your part in learning your lessons now and taking the experience in.

Lessons Summary

- According to Warren Buffett, preparation should be the result of prediction. Knowledge that does not produce action is not worth anything at all.
- Learn from your past mistakes, as well as from the mistakes of others. History repeats itself, and the wise investor will avoid repeat failures.
- Positive habits should be developed early on in life, while bad habits should be corrected while they still can.
- In finances, your savings should be the priority, not the afterthought, according to Buffett. Save first, then spend what is left.
- Buffett highly values the importance of setting time aside to just sit and think. This reduces impulsive decisions.
- He also encourages investors and entrepreneurs to take control of their thoughts through positive self-affirmation.
- Buffett also emphasizes taking care of the body and mind, and investing in oneself as a top priority in order to stay healthy and efficient.
- If you want to grow and develop as a person, you need to keep reading every day, says Buffett.
- The right role models will point you in the right direction, so choose your examples very carefully. Buffett learned from the best.

Conclusion

It is almost certain Warren Buffett will continue to do exactly what he loves to do until the day he regretfully passes from this planet. The truth of the matter is: when you find a burning passion and desire for something, you will want to do it for the rest of your life.

It is one of the many fruitful tips he gives in his infamous lectures, and it is yet another lesson we see played out in his own life.

Long live the Oracle of Omaha.

Thanks for checking out my book. I hope you found this of value and enjoyed it. If this was the case, head to my author page for more like this. Before you go, I have one small favor to ask…

Would you take 60 seconds and write a quick blurb about this book on Amazon?

Reviews are the best way for independent authors (like me) to get noticed, sell more books, and it gives me the motivation to continue producing. I also read every review and use the feedback to write future revisions – and even future books. Thanks again.

Made in the USA
Columbia, SC
17 November 2022

71489072R00052